YOU & YOUR CHILD
LITERACY

Copyright
Every effort has been made to trace copyright holders and to obtain
their permission for the use of copyright material. The authors and
publishers will gladly receive any information enabling them to rectify
any error or omission in subsequent editions.

First published 1999

Letts Educational
Aldine House
Aldine Place
London W12 8AW
Telephone 020 8740 2266

Text: © BPP (Letts Educational) Ltd 1999

Author: Beverley Ann Barnes
Series editor: Roy Blatchford
Project manager: Alex Edmonds
Editorial assistance: Tanya Solomons

Design and illustrations: © BPP (Letts Educational) Ltd 1999
Design by Peter Laws
Illustrations by Madeleine Hardy
Cover design by Peter Laws

British Library Cataloguing in Publication Data
A CIP record for this book is available at the British Library.

ISBN 185758 9742

Colour Reproduction by PDQ Repro Limited, Bungay, Suffolk.
Printed and bound in Italy

Letts Educational is the trading name of BPP (Letts Educational) Ltd

Letts Educational would like to thank all the parents who sent in their tips for educating children
and who wrote with such enthusiasm about parenthood.

YOU & YOUR CHILD
LITERACY

Beverley Ann Barnes

Contents

Words in **bold** are defined in the glossary at the back of this book.

"Do not confine your children to your own learning for they were born in different time."

HEBREW PROVERB

Dear Parent,

What happens at nursery and in primary school is vital to your child's education. What you do at home is just as important.

It's never too soon to start supporting your child's learning. The time that you spend with your child gives him or her a foundation that lasts a lifetime. Make the most of every opportunity for you and your child to enjoy learning together.

You don't need to be an expert. You do need to be enthusiastic. The time you invest at home – sharing picture books and story books, helping with homework, reading and learning together – will give your child the confidence to achieve all through primary and secondary school.

This book is one in a major new series from Letts. It will help you support your child, with information about how children learn to read and write. It tells you how schools help children gain these basic skills, and suggests books for you and your child to share.

The important thing is to make learning fun! I hope you enjoy sharing the gift of reading with your child.

ROY BLATCHFORD
Series editor

What is literacy?

Literacy is the ability to read and write. To be literate your child should be able to understand what he or she has read and be able to explain what his or her own writing means – even if you can't!

Reading: the four strands

Reading is very active. Even the simplest book involves your child in searching for information. When children see words that they have not read before they must work them out. They are often inspired to do this by the desire to know what will happen next in a story.

To be a successful reader your child must:

1   Know the sounds that letters in words make.
    This is called **phonic knowledge**.

2   Recognise whole words. This is called word recognition.

3   Know grammatical rules such as adding an 's' to show more than one. This is called knowledge of **basic grammar**.

4   Be able to use the rest of the text to work out unknown words. This is called knowledge of the context.

Each of these four skills sheds light on the text. The word 'text' is used to refer to whatever your child reads. It could be a story book, a poem or some factual information such as cooking instructions on a tin of beans.

Parent quote

"I encourage my daughter to read by picking books that hold interest for her, such as animal books."

What is phonics?

Phonics is a method of teaching reading based on sounds.

Children are first taught to listen for letter sounds in words. They are then shown how the letters combine to make words by blending – saying the individual sounds in a word and then running them together to make the word. For example, sounding out 'b-a-t' and then saying 'bat'. In school your child will be taught that these sounds are called phonemes.

As your child gets older he or she will be taught to identify more and more complex phonemes such as 'air'. For example, your child will be taught in Year 2, when he or she is six, that the 'air' phoneme can be spelt in several different ways:

'air' in the word 'fair'
'are' in the word 'scare'
'ere' in the word 'there'
'ear' in the word 'bear'

Speaking and listening

Talk is very important to your child's learning. In a child's development, listening comes before talking and talking comes before reading and writing. Literacy develops out of the ability to talk and listen. In school your child's teacher will introduce him or her to reading only after lots of talking and listening work. Talking to your child is very important because:

✔ we all make sense of things by talking about them

✔ talk is used all the time in adult life

✔ talking and listening encourage the development of reading and writing

✔ thinking and co-operation are helped by discussion

Parent quote

"My son started reading a lot more when he found a hobby. I took him to the library to find books on the subject."

Talking

Give your child opportunities to talk about everyday things. You will help him or her to make sense of experiences and remember them. As your child's language develops, thinking develops along with it. If your child uses language readily and easily, he or she will be able to:

✔ Explain what he or she is doing. For example, 'I am making a house with these bricks.'
✔ Describe something he or she wants to do and why. For example, 'I want to paint a picture for my mum for Mothers' Day.'
✔ Ask questions.
✔ Recall a past experience. For example, 'My dad took me to town on Saturday.'
✔ Explain how and why things happen. For example, 'If you blow down your straw you make bubbles in your milk.'

LITERACY IN THE RECEPTION CLASS

When your child joins the Reception class he or she will be introduced to both nursery and modern rhymes, stories, poems, labels and simple non-fiction texts. Week by week your child will be introduced to letters of the alphabet by the sound and the shape of the letters. He or she will be taught a comfortable pencil grip and shown how to write using correct letter formation.

LITERACY AT KEY STAGE ONE

Year 1 (six-year-olds) and Year 2 (seven-year-olds) make up **Key Stage** One. In these years your child will be introduced to a wider range of stories, poetry, simple dictionaries and non-fiction (information) books. **Phonic** work will be continued and your child will be taught to read about 30 common words 'on sight'.

LITERACY AT KEY STAGE TWO

Year 3 (eight-year-olds), Year 4 (nine-year-olds), Year 5 (ten-year-olds) and Year 6 (11-year-olds) make up Key Stage Two. Throughout these years your child will continue to be taught phonic work, spelling, vocabulary and handwriting. The range of fiction, poetry, drama and non-fiction will increase year by year. Your child will study grammar and punctuation every day.

Remember the fun of reading!

By the time they leave primary school children should:

✔ read and write confidently

✔ write in a neat joined-up style

✔ have a large vocabulary

✔ be able to write in different ways, for example stories, reports, instructions, descriptions, arguments

✔ plan and edit their own writing

✔ use grammar and punctuation well

National standards

In primary school your child will take several **National Tests**. Literacy will be tested in the end of Key Stage One assessment in English and the end of Key Stage Two assessment in English. These tests show how your child compares with a child of the same age of average ability. The first test will take place during Year 2 and the second during Year 6.

These tests are very informal and are nothing like the tests that older children take. It is very important that you don't make your child panic. Your child will not be asked to do anything that he or she doesn't do every day in class. Your Year 2 child may not even realise that anything out of the ordinary is going on. The Key Stage One test is done in small groups or with the children working just with the teacher (**teacher assessment**).

What are reading ages?

From time to time you will hear teachers speak of reading ages. If your child is making average progress in reading, his or her reading age will be the same as his or her actual age in years. If your child's reading age is well below his or her age in years it could mean your child has a learning difficulty.

The Literacy Hour

The **Literacy Hour** was introduced to improve literacy standards for all children. It gives teachers a clear framework for teaching the skills of reading and writing. It greatly increases the amount of time the teacher spends teaching the whole class. In every Literacy Hour your child will spend about three quarters of the hour being directly taught by the teacher.

All primary teachers are working from the same handbook, **The National Literacy Strategy Framework for Teaching**. All teachers have taken part in a national training programme which means that wherever your child is at school, he or she is being taught the same knowledge and skills.

Parent quote

"There was so much hype about the Literacy Hour that most parents – including me – were really confused about what it was. Now it seems to be achieving real results."

The Literacy Hour includes:

✔ word work

✔ sentence work

✔ text work

Word work includes:

✔ phonics

✔ spelling and spelling rules

✔ increasing vocabulary

✔ handwriting

Sentence work includes:

✔ grammar

✔ punctuation

Text work includes:

✔ reading comprehension

✔ writing composition

✔ enjoying fiction, poetry and non-fiction

Before your child starts school

Play is of vital importance

You are your child's first and most important teacher. You have a vital part to play in helping your child learn. Play comes naturally to children and is the best way for your child to learn. Play will help your child's mental and physical development. Take every opportunity to play with your child.

From the earliest days your child needs love and stimulation. Help your child to learn by providing toys from the very start. Look for toys that bring new sights, sounds and textures to your baby.

Parent quote

"Before she started school, my daughter knew the alphabet and how to write capital and small letters."

The importance of talk

One of the most important things we do in life is talk. We learn and teach through talking. We share our thoughts and get to know one another through talking. Encourage your child to talk as much as you can. Be a good listener and be interested in what your child says.

Talk with your child at every opportunity. Answer your child's attempts to communicate. Your baby will learn to speak well if:

✔ you expect him or her to speak well

✔ you simplify your talk for your baby

✔ you read to your baby, pointing out pictures

✔ you introduce him or her to rhymes

✔ you talk about shapes, colours and movement as you play with your baby

As your baby develops into a toddler you will be able to have real conversations. As your child's speech develops, the urge to communicate will be even stronger. Talking and listening to your child will be even more enjoyable. Show that you value what he or she says. Do help if he or she gets stuck trying to say something. Toddlers are helped by:

- ✔ being included in plans like arranging a holiday or visit

- ✔ reading and talking about books together

- ✔ being asked lots of questions, especially some that need more than one-word answers

- ✔ watching adults writing

- ✔ being able to link talking and writing, for example talking about what to buy at the shops and making a shopping list

- ✔ saying rhymes with parents or carers

- ✔ being encouraged to talk to other children

- ✔ joining a library

More ideas on how you can help your child

- Encourage your child to tell you what he or she has been doing. As you talk, start to explain the meanings of words.

- Make story-time part of your daily routine. Read a wide range of books, not only stories. Choose information books sometimes, or poetry.

- Listen to stories on tape and follow them in the book.

- Play word games like I Spy.

- Praise your child's attempts to read.

- Sing alphabet songs or teach your child the alphabet. Talk about the names of letters now, not only the sounds of letters.

- Count with your child and talk about numbers, shapes and sizes. Literacy and skills with numbers are closely linked.

- Ask for your child's opinions, and encourage him or her to give full answers by asking lots of 'Why do you think that?' types of questions.

Books for babies

Early contact with books will improve your child's literacy skills. There is no reason why you should not be sharing a book with your baby well before his or her first birthday. When you share a book you are developing a special relationship. This relationship will bring you closer together. You will both enjoy the close contact as you look at books together.

SUITABLE BOOKS FOR BABIES

Books for your baby must be able to stand lots of wear and tear. Board books that are made from sturdy card are excellent. They have rounded corners to make them safe. Board books will withstand chewing, rough handling and dribbling! Cloth books and plastic books for the bath are hard-wearing and fun.

Choose books that are bright, colourful and simple with clear pictures. Your baby will be able to follow what is going on without losing interest. Books like these will provide plenty for you and your baby to talk about. They will encourage lots of pointing and talk. Make sure that the book is of a manageable size. It is important that your baby can hold the book and turn the pages sometimes.

Enjoy your time together.

How to share a book with your baby

Make the time for sharing a book special. Turn off the TV and hi-fi. Sit in a comfortable chair with your baby on your knee. Make sure that your baby can see the book clearly. Make it a happy time with lots of smiles. Point to the pictures and your baby will soon copy you. Talk about the pictures and encourage your baby to join in. Always reply to your baby's sounds.

PHOTOGRAPHIC BOOKS

Babies really enjoy photographs of other babies doing everyday things like playing with toys. Photographs of ordinary and familiar objects help your baby to make a connection between the real world and the printed word.

BOOKS FOR OLDER BABIES

Introduce your baby to a wider range of books. Textured books will encourage your baby to discover how different things feel. Books that make noises will stimulate your baby's curiosity. Your baby will want to hear the sounds over and over again. Your older baby will be enchanted by pop-up books and books with flaps to lift up. Rhymes and stories with repeated words or lines will help your baby to remember the words and join in.

How can I help with early reading?

Your child is beginning to read when he or she realises that words carry meaning and is able to recognise some words. Choose books for a beginning reader which have:

- ✔ simple words
- ✔ clear layout and print
- ✔ repeated words and phrases
- ✔ interesting subjects and settings
- ✔ attractive illustrations

Give your child a variety of books. Let him or her enjoy every page to the full and allow your child to turn the pages. Talk about the pictures and the clues they hold. Ask lots of questions, for example:

? 'What's that called?'

? 'Why do you think she did that?'

? 'What do you think will happen next?'

? 'Which bit did you like best?'

? 'What did you do to work out this word?'

Run your finger under the words as you read them out to reinforce the idea that words carry meaning. When your child joins in and eventually takes over the reading, he or she will copy this.

Teach your child nursery rhymes

Children all over the world love playing with words. They enjoy rhymes, jokes and riddles. This enjoyment encourages children to listen, remember and make the same sound. Being able to recognise the different sounds in words is *very* important when your child is learning to read and write.

Introducing children to rhymes before they go to school gives them a head start. It will make it much easier for them to read and write. Nursery rhymes are simple and repetitive. They give children practice and pleasure in words and their sounds. They help children make an early link between speaking and written language.

Parent tip

"A good starting point is getting your child to write and recognise his or her own name."

How can I help with learning to write?

Help your child to develop good control over his or her hands through playing with toys and games. This important control is called **hand-eye co-ordination**. Jigsaws, bricks and other construction toys like Playmobil and Lego are very good for this. Continue to give lots of opportunities for drawing and colouring using a range of crayons, coloured pencils and paints. As your child starts to recognise letters, encourage him or her to trace over the letters and learn the shapes. Teach your child to write his or her name, starting with a capital letter. Let your child join in with the writing of lists, cards and messages.

Always keep a special time and place to share books. Don't let the phone or TV be a distraction.

Literacy in the Early Years

Nursery schools or nurseries attached to local schools operate on informal lines best suited to the education of the very young. Some state-run nurseries admit children of three years old. The nursery and Reception class together are often referred to as the Early Years. Many areas have Early Years units where both ages are taught together.

Children within the Early Years need to have a wide range of experiences to encourage their language and literacy development. Their teachers plan these around six broad areas of learning:

- ✔ language and literacy

- ✔ mathematics

- ✔ personal and social development

- ✔ knowledge and understanding of the world

- ✔ creative development

- ✔ physical development

> **Parent tip**
>
> "A fun game is to cut words up and get your child to put them together like a jigsaw."

Many activities are set up to aid your child's development in each of these areas. Literacy is an important factor in all of them.

In the classroom

Here are some examples of the types of things going on in parts of the nursery classroom or Early Years unit.

You would usually find the room or rooms divided into areas devoted to particular activities:

- Interactive displays (lots of things for children to look at, touch and explore)

- Outside play/gardening

- Mark making (pencils, pens, letters, letter stamps, paper, card etc.)

- Jigsaws, puzzles and board games

- Music

- Food technology/snack making

- Modelling

- Construction (bricks, Lego etc)

- Stories, puppets, book area, listening centre

- Water and sand play

- Paint, collage and wood

- Role play and home play

In the nursery setting most of the work is done in small groups or on an individual basis. This is the best way to teach three- and four-year-old children. In the school term after your child is five he or she will enter the slightly more formal world of the Reception class.

What your child will be expected to be able to do on entering the Reception class

The age at which your child will enter the Reception class can be different depending on where you live. In some areas your child will go into Reception at the age of four, while in other areas it won't be until the term after his or her fifth birthday.

The Reception class teacher will be able to teach your child best if he or she is able to do certain things, covered by the broad headings:

✔ speaking and listening

✔ reading

✔ writing

Reception year literacy

In the Reception class the teacher will teach the whole class together on many more occasions than in the nursery. In the term before your child goes into the Year 1 class (at the age of six) he or she will be doing a full Literacy Hour every day.

A detailed description of how the hour works is in the next chapter.

SPEAKING AND LISTENING

Your child should be able to listen with attention and talk about everyday experiences in a small or a large group. He or she should also be able to listen to and enjoy stories, songs, rhymes and poems. Being able to make up stories and take part in role play or acting out is also expected.

READING

At this stage, your child's reading skills should include the ability to:

> **Parent quote**
>
> "My children love to make words with alphabet pasta."

- ✔ enjoy books, handle them carefully and understand how they are read
- ✔ recognise his or her own name and some familiar words
- ✔ recognise the letters of the alphabet by their shape and sound
- ✔ understand that words and pictures have meaning
- ✔ understand that, in English, the print is read from left to right and from top to bottom
- ✔ pick out sound patterns in rhymes and begin to associate sounds with syllables, words and letters

WRITING

At this stage your child's writing skills should include the ability to:

- ✔ use familiar words, letters, pictures and symbols to communicate meaning
- ✔ understand that there are different reasons for writing, for example a parent writing a note to the teacher or someone writing a book
- ✔ write his or her own name, starting with a capital letter.

Your child will learn to make sense of the world through language.

Shared Reading

Through shared reading, when the whole class and the teacher read a book together, your child will be able to:

✔ recognise hand-written and printed words, for example in stories, notes, labels, signs, forms, letters, directions, lists, advertisements, newspapers

✔ understand and use correctly words to describe books and print: *book, cover, beginning, end, page, line, word, letter, title*

✔ follow text in the right order, from left to right, from top to bottom, page by page and knowing that each written word has a corresponding spoken word

Through the experience of shared reading your child will also practise the following skills:

✔ using clues from the context of a story to work out new words

✔ being able to use story book language when re-telling stories, e.g. 'Once there was…', 'She lived in a little cottage….', 'he cried'

✔ re-reading familiar texts e.g. Big Books, story books, taped stories with texts, poems, information books, his or her own and other children's writing

✔ using his or her knowledge of familiar texts to act out or re-tell to others the main points in the right order

✔ being able to find and read special parts of a text e.g. captions, names of characters, rhymes and repeated parts, e.g. 'You can't catch me, I'm the Gingerbread Man…'

✔ knowing how stories are built up with one event following another and the final outcome or ending

✔ re-reading and telling 'off by heart' stories and rhymes with predictable and repeated words

What writing will my child do in the Reception class?

Your child will be encouraged to experiment with writing and always 'have a go' at what he or she wants to write. This will include practising writing his or her own name regularly and writing labels for pictures and drawings. The teacher will help your child to think and talk about what he or she wants to write before starting. All the texts that the class share with the teacher – the stories, poems and simple information texts – will be a good foundation for this independent writing.

Why have a Literacy Hour?

At school, reading and writing are so important that it is a sensible idea to have a set time for teaching them every day. The teacher can teach all the children important knowledge and skills at the same time. Children learn a lot from listening to one another. This happens all through the Literacy Hour.

Children in the Reception class are very gradually introduced to the Literacy Hour. From the time your child starts Year 1 he or she will be doing a full Literacy Hour every day of the week. This will continue right up to the time your child leaves Year 6.

What happens in a Literacy Hour?

All the time in the Literacy Hour is spent on reading and writing. The hour is divided into four parts. For the first 15 minutes or so the whole class works together on shared reading or writing. The next 15 minutes are spent on phonics, spelling, vocabulary, grammar or punctuation. During the next 20 minutes the class works in groups and the teacher teaches reading to one of the groups. Finally, the whole class comes back together and spends about ten minutes discussing what has been learned in the lesson.

Whole class talking about what has been learned

Whole class shared reading or writing

Group and individual guided reading and writing

Whole class word and sentence work

The first 15 minutes: shared reading and writing

In Reception, Year 1 and Year 2 your child's teacher may use a Big Book for the shared reading part of the Literacy Hour. A Big Book is simply a book that is larger than normal. The teacher uses it so that all the children in the class can see easily.

The teacher will start by reading the book aloud and pointing to the words and pictures. He or she will read it again and the children will be asked to join in if they want to. The teacher asks questions to encourage the children to think about what they read, for example, 'What do you think will happen next?' or, 'What does that word mean?'. She might ask a child to point out where the title of the book is or why a specific part of the story is funny. Some questions will be very simple. In this way all the children are fully involved, from the most to the least able. The teacher adapts the questions to suit the different abilities of the children in the class. This method of teaching is called differentiation. All the children gain confidence and they can learn a lot from each other.

The teacher's questions help the children to understand the meaning of the text. On some days the teacher will concentrate on writing. He or she will show the class how to write by writing words on the board. They could be working on a story, poem or piece of information writing. In this way the teacher demonstrates good writing. This does not mean just good handwriting but how to plan what you want to write, organise it and make any changes.

The teacher will also teach the class many early reading and writing skills. Examples of what he or she will teach them include:

✔ learning that words go from left to right

✔ understanding how to use full stops, capital letters and other punctuation

✔ recognising letters and words

✔ hearing the sounds of letters

✔ hearing sounds or words that rhyme

Parent quote

"I still remember how pleased we were to see Robert pick up a book and read on his own for the first time. The years of reading to him really paid off."

How will I know what progress my child is making?

Your child's teacher will invite you into school to discuss progress at set times during the year. Schools are happy to talk to parents about their children's progress at other times, as long as you make an appointment to do so. Your child's teacher will also set targets that your child can work towards.

When your child moves on to Key Stage Two he or she will be able to read and write much more independently. It is said that your child is becoming an independent reader and writer. In Years 3, 4, 5 and 6 your child will still do a Literacy Hour every day. The difference is that he or she will work on more difficult books and different kinds of books. Every term your child will read information books, stories, poems, plays, biographies and reports. In the Literacy Hour in Key Stage Two your child will learn how to spell more difficult words. He or she will learn how to put sentences and paragraphs together.

The next 15 minutes: word and sentence work

In Key Stage One the next 15 minutes or so will be taken up with work that concentrates on words. Your child will be learning phonics (the sounds in words), how to recognise whole words, the meanings of words and handwriting. In Key Stage Two the work will include grammar and punctuation.

The next 20 minutes: guided reading and writing

The next 20 minutes or so will be spent on group work. The teacher will decide the best number of groups for his or her particular class and how many children will be in each group. There should not be more than six children in a group. Each day the teacher works with one or two different groups for guided reading or writing. All the children in the class will have been taught to work on their own and get on independently.

Sometimes groups in class will be set by ability in order to challenge all children.

For a child in Reception, learning targets might be:

✔ to learn six letters of the alphabet

✔ to read and write his or her own name

✔ to re-tell a story in his or her own words

During a Literacy Hour, the teacher will work with your child's group for at least 20 minutes each week. Your child will be doing reading and writing work linked exactly to his or her ability. Each child will have his or her own copy of the same book and the teacher will be able to give full attention to the group that he or she is teaching. In guided reading sessions the teacher will be teaching your child to read rather than just hearing your child read.

Parent quote

"My son's school provides a reading diary which myself, my son and his teacher write in. They also send plenty of books home."

In the Reception class, your child will learn to:

✔ expect text to make sense and to check if it does not

✔ use clues from the story, pictures, grammar and phonics to help with reading

By the time he or she is in Year 6 your child will learn to:

✔ investigate the author's point of view

✔ refer to the text for evidence to back up opinions

The last 10 minutes: the plenary

For a child in Year 6 targets might be:

✔ to learn a particular spelling rule

✔ to understand how to use a semi-colon

✔ to tell the difference between fact, opinion and fiction

You can help your child reach the targets by practising with him or her and praising achievements. There will be other ways that you can help. The school may send books home and ask you to read them with your child. You will be invited to meet your child's teacher to look at his or her work and discuss progress.

If your child's school has a homework policy, it will be explained to you. The school will ask for your support in making sure homework is done.

In the last part of the Literacy Hour the teacher works with the whole class again. This part is called the plenary, meaning group work. He or she will go over what was taught during the first half hour, highlighting the main points. The teacher will ask lots of questions and encourage the children to talk about what they did and what they found out while they were working independently. Children are expected to listen carefully to others in their class.

Literacy at Key Stage One

Year 1 (five-and six-year-olds) and Year 2 (six-and seven-year-olds) are the infant years – Key Stage One. Towards the end of Year 2 in the **National Curriculum**, children will take a National Test in English, called the end of Key Stage One assessment. The test is made up of sections on reading, writing and spelling. Children are given a level according to how they do in the test.

✔ Most seven-year-olds are expected to reach Level 2a or 2b.

✔ Some very able children reach Level 3 which is better than that expected of seven-year-olds.

Parent quote

"We thought that English was only taught in the Literacy Hour, but Pete's teacher told us that English is taught in many different ways and literacy itself is an important aspect of all subjects."

The National Literacy Strategy Framework for Teaching

The government has produced a detailed document for teachers called The National Literacy Strategy Framework for Teaching. It sets out clearly what is to be taught in literacy and when. It also indicates what types of literature such as stories, poems, information texts, plays and so on are to be studied. The National Numeracy Strategy does a similar thing for the teaching of mathematics in schools.

Summary of the work taught in Year 1, term 1

What will my child be doing in Year 1, term 1?

Children will be introduced to stories with familiar settings and stories and rhymes with predictable and repetitive patterns. They will be looking at words on labels, signs, captions, lists and instructions.

WORD LEVEL WORK

Your child will be taught to play with rhyming patterns such as *fat* and *hat*. He or she will practise the alphabet, learn simple words, such as *mat*, and learn to recognise familiar words such as children's names and labels. He or she will learn to write small (lower case) letters.

SENTENCE LEVEL WORK

This will include making sense of what he or she reads and writing captions and small sentences. He or she will learn to recognise full stops and capital letters and sentences.

Parent quote

"We found that Edward was beginning to have a lot more interest in his books around Year 1. Whereas before he'd not thought about what the characters were wearing or why they did what they did, it suddenly became important to him and he was constantly asking 'Why?'."

TEXT LEVEL WORK

This will include reading simple familiar stories and describing the settings of the stories. Your child's teacher might get him or her to make simple picture books.

In Year 1 your child will be building on the work done in the Reception class.

What will my child be doing in Year 1, term 2?

In fiction and poetry he or she will be reading traditional stories and rhymes as well as fairy stories. The stories and poems come from a range of cultures and have predictable and repeated rhymes. In non-fiction he or she will be looking at information books, reports and dictionaries.

Summary of the work taught in Year 1, term 2

WORD LEVEL WORK

In word level work your child will investigate and read more complicated words such as those ending in *ff, ll* or *ck*.

SENTENCE LEVEL WORK

In sentence level work your child will practise a lot of the work he or she learned in the previous term.

TEXT LEVEL WORK

In text level work your child will learn how to re-tell stories, giving the major points as well as talking about why things happened in stories. He or she will also talk about the characters in stories and understand the difference between fiction and non-fiction.

Literacy out of hours

Teachers will continue to check on your child's progress outside the Literacy Hour. Reading, learning drama or how to write stories all help to develop your child's literacy skills.

Summary of the work taught in Year 1, term 3

WORD LEVEL WORK

This will look at the different ways of spelling the same sounds, such as 'ee' which can be spelt as 'ee' in feet or 'ea' in seat. Your child will also learn what vowels and consonants are.

SENTENCE LEVEL WORK

In sentence level work he or she will become more familiar with using capital letters and learn about question marks.

TEXT LEVEL WORK

Text level work will look at how titles, pictures, covers and information on the back of a book can tell us what stories are about. Your child will also learn how to write about his or her own experiences.

Summary of the work taught in Year 2, term 1

What will my child be doing in Year 2, term 1?

In fiction and poetry he or she will be reading stories and poems with familiar settings. In non-fiction he or she will be looking at instructions, such as recipes.

Your child will also be taught to unde marks and commas when reading.

TEXT LEVEL WORK

Text level work looks at the reason wl stories, memorising favourite poems a writing simple instructions.

WORD LEVEL WORK

Word level work in Year 2 begins with looking at common spelling patterns and basic handwriting joins.

SENTENCE LEVEL WORK

Sentence level work looks at

Summary of the work taught in Year 2, term 2

What will my child be doing in Year 2, term 2?

In fiction and poetry your child will be reading traditional stories and stories and poems from other cultures. These stories will have predictable and patterned language. Children will also look at poems by famous children's poets.

In non-fiction your child will be using dictionaries, glossaries and indexes.

WORD LEVEL WORK

Word level work in term 2 of Year 2 looks at common spelling patterns and words containing 'wh', 'ph' and 'ch'.

SENTENCE LEVEL WORK

Sentence level work concentrates on using commas to separate items on a list. Your child will learn how to predict story endings in text level work as well as reading his or her own poems out loud and talking about favourite poems and poets. He or she will learn to write simple character descriptions and how to use dictionaries and glossaries to find words. Your child will also learn to produce simple flow charts and diagrams to explain how things happen in books.

Parent quote

"Far from finding it daunting, when we looked at the break down of what Katie was learning each term, it really helped us to back up her school work with home learning."

Summary of the work taught in Year 2, term 3

What will my child be doing in Year 2, term 3?

In fiction and poetry children will be reading longer stories by famous children's authors. They will read different stories by the same author and compare them. Children are taught language play, for example riddles, tongue-twisters, humorous verse and stories.

WORD LEVEL WORK

In term 3 your child will learn to spell and read words containing 'ear' and 'ea' sounds such as 'ear' in *fear* and *hear* and 'ea' in *bread* and *head*.

SENTENCE LEVEL WORK

Sentence level work will teach your child to turn statements into questions using 'what', 'where', 'when' and 'who'.

TEXT LEVEL WORK

In text level work your child will compare books by the same author and learn to glean information about authors from book covers. He or she will practise writing short evaluations of books and will write non-fiction using headings and captions. In non-fiction he or she will read information books including reports.

What should my child be able to do by the end of Key Stage One?

By the end of Key Stage One most children should be able to read independently. They should be able to tackle many unfamiliar texts with confidence, correcting themselves when they make mistakes. They should be using a range of clues to work out how to read unfamiliar words. Children should be able to write quite long pieces of work. They should have learnt to recognise that there may be more than one way to make a particular sound. Word level work of this kind helps with reading and writing.

When teachers help children they should be tactful and responsive to children's attempts. With similar support from home your child will be well prepared to enter Key Stage Two, the junior years.

Throughout Key Stage One the teachers will be directly teaching all aspects of literacy. They will also pay careful attention to each child's individual needs and note signs of progress.

Parent quote

"I'd never enjoyed poetry myself, but when Ali brought home his poetry books we all really enjoyed reading them together."

How can I help my child with spelling, writing and reading?

Good spelling is not a sign of intelligence and poor spelling is nothing to do with being lazy. If your child has difficulty with certain words again and again try different ideas to help him or her remember. Be very careful not to confuse or overload your child with too much at once.

✔ Look for tricks to help them remember words they have difficulty with. These little tricks are called mnemonics (pronounced nee-mon-ics).

Some people remember how to spell necessary by saying, 'one collar, two sleeves'. This is a mnemonic. This one will help your child to remember how to spell 'guard': teach him or her to say 'Give uncle Arthur red dates.'

Spelling tips

✔ Teach your child some spelling rules such as 'q is always followed by u'.

✔ Another simple spelling rule is that if you can hear an 'e' or an 'i' sound at the end of a word it will almost always be spelt with a 'y' – for example, *try, my, family, happy, chemistry*.

✔ The 'i before e except after c' rule is a good one to remember. It holds true most of the time – receipt, ceiling – but not for seize and several other words.

✔ You may know other rules yourself, or you can find them in a book on spelling.

What to look for in your child's handwriting

Do not compare your child's handwriting with other children's. We are all individuals with different talents. Here are some questions to ask yourself as you look.

- ✔ Are the letters more or less the same size?

- ✔ Are the spaces between letters even and the spaces between words even?

- ✔ Is your child using the correct joins?

- ✔ Does your child's writing flow evenly or is it jerky?

- ✔ Can you read what has been written?

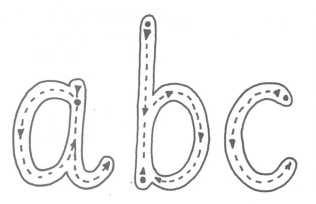

There is a correct way to form each letter of the alphabet.

Spelling rules

There are many spelling rules in English but few work all the time. If the rule causes confusion, stop teaching the rule. When you help your child with spelling it will help most if it is interesting. The more fun involved the better.

Children have a natural interest in words that you can make use of as a parent. Tests are fine but they do not teach your child spellings.

Parent quote

"We realised just how much handwriting teaching had changed when Luke brought his books home."

How to help your child with handwriting

By giving your child toys and writing materials at home you have given him or her a great start to handwriting. From their early 'pretend' writing or mark making, handwriting will emerge. The mixture of scribble, pretend and practice writing that children produce is called emergent writing.

When you show your pre-school child how to write, do not use capital (upper case) letters. Children are taught from Year 1 onwards how to write letters that will be easy to join later. This means writing letters with small kicks or tails on them, rather than the 'stick and ball' printing of previous generations. From Year 2 (six- to seven-year-olds) onwards children are taught how to join their letters.

Teach your child to relax when writing

Your child's legs should not be crossed when he or she writes and his or her feet should be on the floor. Make sure that he or she does not hunch up the shoulders. Encourage your child to shake his or her hands before writing so that the hands feel really floppy. If your child feels discomfort when holding a pencil or pen talk to the teacher.

The right conditions for writing

When children write, whether at home or at school, it is very important that:

✎ they can see what they are writing

✎ they have a desk or table that is the right height for them

✎ they have their book or paper in the best position for them

✎ they have a pencil or pen that suits them

✎ they hold their pencil or pen in a comfortable way that lets their fingers move easily

✎ they have a clear and tidy desk or table

The position of the paper is important

If your child is right–handed he or she should place the paper or book to the right of the centre line of his or her body. If your child is left–handed he or she should place the paper or book to the left of the centre line of his or her body. Your child's hand and forearm should rest on the table.

If your child is left–handed you can help by:

✎ making sure that your child sits to the left of tables and double desks so that he or she does not bump elbows with right-handed neighbours

✎ making sure that your child puts the paper on the left–hand side then slants it to suit his or her individual needs

✎ making sure that the seat is high enough so that your child can see over his or her hand

✎ making sure that the lighting is good so that he or she isn't writing in the hand's shadow

✎ making sure that your child grips the pencil or pen higher than a right-handed child, to stop the writing hand blocking out what has been written

✎ making sure that fountain pens are not used too soon. Your left–handed child has his or her hand following the pen, so smudging is likely

✎ providing a roller-ball type pen which will make writing much easier

> ### Left-handers
>
> It is perfectly natural to be left-handed. About one in ten of the population is left-handed. Sometimes left-handed people produce mirror writing. Don't worry, this is completely natural for left-handers. There are specialist shops selling equipment adapted for left-handed people.

How to hear your child read

Most children enjoy reading to adults. Grandparents, aunts, uncles, carers, family friends all have a part to play. Build on this enjoyment. Try not to make your child read to you if he or she is involved in another enjoyable activity. Make reading part of your daily routine so that you can both plan for it and look forward to it. Make sure that you can both see the book properly and are comfortable. Talk about the book first; ask questions about it such as:

'Why did you choose this book?'

'What do you think this book is going to be about?'

It is not always necessary to point out every mistake. For example, if your child's reading makes sense but he or she adds an occasional extra word, don't bother to correct it. If he or she keeps on doing it, get him or her to read again, pointing to every word.

Don't worry if your child brings the same book home from school from time to time. Familiar reading is very important for building up confidence and fluency. If your child always has books that are difficult he or she will see reading as a struggle and avoid it.

At the end of the reading session, always try to praise something about your child's reading, for example:

'I like the way you correct yourself when you read.'

'You read with really good expression now.'

'You have improved in your reading!'

The time that you spend listening will depend on the two of you. Some children will happily read for half an hour at a time. You might not have that much time to spend with him or her. A little and often is of far more benefit than an occasional long read.

When your child meets a word that he or she cannot read, try the following things:

✍ If the word can be guessed from the picture, encourage him or her to have a guess.

✍ If the word can be guessed from what he or she has already read, encourage your child to have a go.

✍ Tell him or her to read on to the end of the sentence and then have a go.

✍ Help your child to see that he or she knows the biggest parts of the word already (for example, jump-ing, walk-ed) by breaking it into parts. If he or she reads the familiar part, it can be finished off letter by letter.

✍ If a word can be sounded out, encourage him or her to do that.

✍ If it is a word that he or she has never met before or an unusual name, just give your child the word.

> **Parent quote**
>
> "When I'm travelling home on the train, I start to think about cuddling up with my son for 'milk and stories'. We both love it!"

Literacy at Key Stage Two

Years 3, 4, 5 and 6 make up Key Stage Two. Your child will be between seven and 11 years old. In Year 6 your child will take a National Test in English called the end of Key Stage Two assessment. Your child may not have had his or her 11th birthday when the test takes place.

All children who can cope with the questions take the test. There are sections on reading, writing, handwriting and spelling. As in Key Stage One children are given a level showing how they did in the test.

✔ Most 11-year-olds are expected to reach Level 4.

✔ Some very able children reach Level 5 which is better than that expected of 11-year-olds.

Shared reading and writing

Through the careful conversations that the class and the teacher will have about texts in shared reading within the Literacy Hour, your child will become a more thoughtful reader and writer. To make sure that your child can become an accurate speller he or she will be taught spelling until the end of Year 6. Your child will be taught patterns of spelling and the different ways some sounds can be spelled.

What literacy work will my child do in Key Stage Two?

In Key Stage Two – the junior years – children will be introduced to a widening range of books. They will be encouraged to consult different sources of information in all the subjects that they study. This is why literacy is so important. Chidren who experience difficulties with reading and writing will be prevented from doing their best in other subjects too. Key Stage Two teachers will also help your child to develop ideas and organise his or her writing. This will mean that he or she can express thoughts and choose words with care.

Summary of the work taught in Year 3, term 1

What will my child be doing in Year 3, term 1?

In fiction and poetry children will be studying stories with familiar settings. They will read plays, and poems that are based on observation and the senses. They will look at shape poems – literally poems written in shapes. In non-fiction they will be looking at information books on topics of interest, reports and continue working with thesauruses and dictionaries.

WORD LEVEL WORK

Word level work includes children identifying mis-spelt words in their own work and practising spellings by looking at words, saying the words, covering them up, writing them out and checking what they've written – the Look, Say, Cover, Write and Check method.

SENTENCE LEVEL WORK

Sentence level work concentrates on teaching them verbs. They are taught to express their own views on a story or poem in text level work and they will also begin to organise stories into paragraphs.

Summary of the work taught in Year 3, term 2

What will my child be doing in Year 3, term 2?

In fiction and poetry children will be reading myths, legends, fables and parables. They will also look at traditional stories with similar themes and oral and performance poetry from different cultures.

In non-fiction they will continue to look at instructions, dictionaries without illustrations and thesauruses.

WORD LEVEL WORK

Word level work includes words with silent letters such as 'knee', 'gnat' and 'wrinkle'. Children are also taught to understand what a definition is.

SENTENCE LEVEL WORK

Sentence level work includes learning about adjectives.

TEXT LEVEL WORK

Text level work encourages children to find the themes in stories and make clear notes.

What will my child be doing in Year 3, term 3?

In fiction and poetry children will be studying adventure and mystery stories as well as continuing work on different stories by the same author. Children are introduced to humorous poetry and poetry that plays with language as well as word puzzles, puns and riddles.

In non-fiction children will be learning about letters written for various reasons – to explain, enquire, congratulate, complain. Teachers introduce alphabetic texts, directories, encyclopedias and indexes.

Summary of the work taught in term 3

In word level work children learn to use apostrophes to spell shortened or contracted words like 'couldn't'. They learn about homonyms (words that are spelled the same but with different meanings) such as 'form' meaning a bench, a class or a document. Sentence level work includes pronouns and speech marks. In text level work children write book reviews and letters.

Summary of the work taught in Year 4, term 2

What will my child be doing in Year 4, term 1?

In fiction and poetry children will be studying historical stories and short novels as well as playscripts. They will read poems based on themes such as space, school, animals, families or feelings.

In non-fiction they will be looking at reports, articles in newspapers and magazines and instructions.

WORD LEVEL WORK

Word work at this stage looks at placing words in alphabetical order.

SENTENCE LEVEL WORK

In sentence level work children are taught that tenses are about time – the past tense, present tense and future tense. They also learn adverbs.

TEXT LEVEL WORK

In text level work children are shown how to plan out the main stages of a story. They use paragraphs and future tenses in this work. They also continue practising writing instructions.

Parent quote

"We were really worried that our grammar wasn't up to scratch when Eve got to Year 4, but we all mucked in and I think it helped her a bit knowing that we were really learning too."

Summary of the work taught in Year 4, term 2

What will my child be doing in Year 4, term 2?

In fiction and poetry children will be reading stories and novels about imagined worlds, science fiction, fantasy adventures and stories in series.

They are taught classic and modern poetry, including poetry from different cultures and times.

In non-fiction they will continue to look at information books on the same or similar themes.

WORD LEVEL WORK

In word level work children are taught to spell words with common endings, such as 'ight' in *fight*, *sight* and *light*. The class are taught to appreciate that vocabulary changes over time and that some words, such as 'wireless', are not used much anymore.

SENTENCE LEVEL WORK

In sentence level work children learn to use the apostrophe to signal possession, for example 'the man's hat', meaning the hat that the man owns.

TEXT LEVEL WORK

Text level work includes building an understanding of how expressive and descriptive language can create moods or build tension.

Summary of the work taught in Year 4, term 3

What will my child be doing in Year 4, term 3?

In fiction and poetry children will be studying stories and short novels that raise issues such as bullying, death or injustice. They will continue to work on stories by the same author and stories from other cultures. They work on many different types of poetry in different forms such as haiku (a Japanese form of poetry based on syllable patterns), cinquain (poetry based on a five-line syllable pattern), lists, rhyming forms and free verse (poetry which is not restricted to patterns of rhymes and rhythm).

WORD LEVEL WORK

Word level work looks at spelling words that have the same letters but different pronunciations, such as 'tough', 'through', 'trough' and 'hour'.

SENTENCE LEVEL WORK

In sentence level work children are taught to react to punctuation marks, such as commas, semi-colons, dashes, hyphens and speech marks, when reading.

TEXT LEVEL WORK

In text level work children are shown how to identify social, moral or cultural issues in stories. They are asked to write alternative endings to stories and to summarise a sentence or paragraph in a set number of words. They also learn how to present a point of view in writing.

Parent quote

"Like many parents, we were not familiar with some of the more unusual forms of poetry. But there is no doubt that poetry has helped our child to express her thoughts and choose her words with care."

Summary of the work taught in Year 5, term 1

WORD LEVEL WORK

Word level work includes looking at where words came from, and at spelling patterns such as 'sign', 'signature' and 'signal'.

SENTENCE LEVEL WORK

In sentence level work they will analyse how dialogue is set out.

TEXT LEVEL WORK

They will write new scenes or characters into an existing story as well as learning to use simple abbreviations in note-taking.

Parent tip

"Our family loves Scrabble and Hangman – they are fun to play and they stimulate an interest in letters and words."

Summary of the work taught in Year 5, term 2

What will my child be doing in Year 5, term 2?

In fiction, children will be looking at traditional stories, myths, legends and fables from a range of cultures. In poetry they will be studying longer classic poems.

Their non-fiction work will be based on non-chronological reports (writing which describes rather than journalistic, newspaper writing) and explanations.

WORD LEVEL WORK

Some of the word level work involves children investigating homophones (words with the same pronunciation but different spellings, for example 'rain', 'rein' or 'reign') and onomatopeia (where the meaning of a word is represented by its sound, for example 'splash', 'plop' and 'swoop').

SENTENCE LEVEL WORK

In sentence level work children will learn about double meaning or ambiguity. For example, does the sign that says 'Baby Changing Room' indicate the room where babies' nappies can be changed or the room where one baby can be changed for another baby? They will practise using commas to make the meaning of long, complex sentences clear.

Summary of the work taught in Year 5, term 3

What will my child be doing in Year 5, term 3?

In fiction and poetry children will be studying novels, stories and poems from a variety of cultures and traditions. They will also work with choral and performance poetry.

In non-fiction they will be using persuasive writing to put forward or argue a point of view through letters, commentaries or leaflets to persuade, criticise, protest, support, object and complain. They will also be learning more about dictionaries and thesauruses, including I.C.T. sources such as CD-ROMs.

WORD LEVEL WORK

In this term's word work children learn about how certain words, such as khaki and bungalow, are borrowed from foreign languages.

SENTENCE LEVEL WORK

In sentence level work children will learn about clauses.

TEXT LEVEL WORK

In text level work they learn how to write in the style of an author and learn how to try to persuade other classmates round to their point of view by making a good, solid argument and presenting it.

Summary of the work taught in Year 6, term 1

What will my child be doing in Year 6, term 1?

In fiction and poetry children will be studying classic fiction, poetry and drama by long-established authors including, where appropriate, study of a Shakespeare play and adaptations of classics on film and television.

In non-fiction they will be looking at autobiographies and biographies, diaries, journals, letters, anecdotes, records of observations and journalistic writing.

WORD AND SENTENCE LEVEL WORK

Children continue their previous work in word level and sentence level work.

TEXT LEVEL WORK

In text level work they summarise passages or chapters of text in a set number of words as well as learning to write in a journalistic style.

Summary of the work taught in Year 6, term 2

What will my child be doing in Year 6, term 2?

In fiction they will continue to look at a variety of different novel styles. In poetry they will study and compare many different types of poem.

In non-fiction they will be looking at discussion texts that set out, balance and weigh up different points of view. They will look at formal writing such as public information notices and documents.

WORD LEVEL WORK

Children are taught to explain the meanings of proverbs such as 'too many cooks spoil the broth'.

SENTENCE LEVEL WORK

In sentence level work they begin to understand the difference between active and passive verbs, for example, 'Tom ate the cake' (active verb) and 'The cake was eaten by Tom' (passive verb).

TEXT LEVEL WORK

In text level work children learn how to build up a good argument and how to write a balanced report.

Summary of the work taught in Year 6, term 3

What will my child be doing in Year 6, term 3?

In this term children continue to look at and enjoy reading famous authors.

In non-fiction they will be looking at explanations of ideas and reports linked to work from other subjects . They will continue to read reference texts, dictionaries and thesauruses and to use I.C.T. sources.

WORD LEVEL WORK

Children are taught to experiment with language by creating new words in word level work.

SENTENCE LEVEL WORK

In sentence level work they continue to explore language by looking at dialect, proverbs and how language develops.

TEXT LEVEL WORK

In text level work they look in detail at the work of one writer and how it changes over time.

What should my child be able to do by the end of Key Stage Two?

By now your child should be reading and writing confidently. He or she should recognise most words on sight and be able to work out unknown words, correcting him or herself when necessary. At the end of this Key Stage, children should be spelling accurately and writing in a smooth and joined-up style. Most children have a growing vocabulary and an interest in words and their meanings at this stage.

As you look through your child's work you should be able to see examples of many different types of writing, for example stories, poems, letters, plays, reports, arguments and persuasive pieces. You should also be able to see evidence of planning, revising and editing of work. Your child should be able to use quite advanced technical vocabulary to talk about his or her literacy work. Reading and writing should have developed

What if my child has special educational needs?

Many children have special educational needs. This means that they have a learning difficulty that needs special teaching. A child with a learning difficulty has more problems learning than other children of the same age. Most children with special educational needs do not go to special schools. They are taught successfully in the classrooms of mainstream schools. It is estimated that 20% of children need special educational help at some stage in their school lives.

Teachers are able to recognise children who experience learning difficulties by looking for the following signs:

✔ they may not have made a start at all in classwork

✔ they may have fallen behind their classmates in reading and writing

✔ they may have begun to learn to read and write but are not picking up new skills as quickly as other children

Many children in ordinary classrooms have special educational needs. If your child finds reading and writing more difficult than most of the other children in the class the teacher will make an Individual Education Plan. This is designed to allow your child to get the greatest benefit from every lesson. The work will be broken down into the exact steps your child needs.

READING

If at the end of Year One your child:

✘ has no knowledge of books or cannot share a book

✘ cannot recognise 20 common words

✘ has little or no knowledge of the first sound of words

✘ does not know when words rhyme

then it is likely that your child has a learning difficulty.

If at the end of Year Two he or she:

✘ cannot recognise when two or more letters blend together to make one sound, for example 'st' or 'th'

✘ is not making good progress with the graded reading books used by the school

✘ is reading below the level of the average five and a half-year-old

then it is likely that your child has a learning difficulty.

WRITING

If at the end of Year 1 your child:

    ✗ does not understand what writing is for

    ✗ does not do any mark making or pretend writing

    ✗ is not able to write his or her own name

it is likely that he or she has a learning difficulty in writing.

If at the end of Year 2 your child:

    ✗ does not try to write in simple sentences

    ✗ only uses the most simple words in his or her writing

it is likely that he or she has a learning difficulty in writing.

SPELLING

If your child is in Year 2 or above and:

    ✗ cannot spell the simplest three-letter words, for
       example 'cat', 'dog' or 'ran'

    ✗ cannot remember how to spell simple words he or she has been
       taught

it is likely that he or she has a learning difficulty in spelling.

If your child is in Year 3 or above and:

    ✗ makes mistakes with most of the letters he or she writes

    ✗ has handwriting that is impossible to read

    ✗ writes very slowly – about ten letters a minute

it is likely that he or she has a learning difficulty in spelling.

What is dyslexia?

Dyslexia is a particular learning difficulty that makes learning to read and write harder than for most people. It has nothing to do with intelligence – people of all intellectual levels can be dyslexic. Dyslexia runs in families and about three times as many boys as girls are affected.

Skilled teachers can do a great deal to help dyslexic pupils. Children with dyslexia can be very hurt and frustrated if they are treated as lazy. If your child is dyslexic you must do all you can to make sure it does not damage his or her confidence and self-esteem.

Differentiation

If your child finds aspects of reading or writing difficult it is important not to worry him or her. The teacher will break the work down into steps that your child can cope with. During the first 30 minutes of the Literacy Hour, when the whole class is taught together, your child's teacher will involve all the children by asking the right questions of each individual child – this is called differentiation. More able children may be asked different questions from children with special needs.

Recognising dyslexia

If you answer 'Yes' to most of the following questions, you should ask for advice. But speak with your child's teacher first. If the teacher is worried he or she will speak to the school's special educational needs co-ordinator who may call in professional help, if necessary.

AT ALL AGES:

- Is your child bright in some ways but makes no progress in others?
- Is there anyone else in the family with difficulties like this?

SOME EARLY SYMPTOMS:

- Does your child find it hard to remember two or more instructions in order?
- Can he or she manipulate things like Lego very well but is clumsy in other ways?
- Is your child not sure which hand to use for eating?
- Does your child have difficulty getting dressed, put clothes on in the wrong order or have problems with buttons and laces?
- Does he or she get the names of things mixed up?
- Does your child say things back to front such as 'par cark' instead of 'car park'? This is called a spoonerism.
- Does your child find it hard to remember nursery rhymes?

How parents can help at home

It is important that parents are encouraging and praise whenever possible. Always find something that your child is good at. Make sure you set aside time to read with your child. Help your child to discover personal interests. Introduce your child to art, nature, music, museums and sport. Ask the school to suggest homework activities. By doing these things you will help your child whatever his or her level of ability.

CHILDREN AGED SEVEN TO 11 YEARS OLD

- Does your child have particular difficulty with reading or spelling?
- Does your child often put letters or numbers the wrong way round, for example '51' instead of '15', 'd' instead of 'b', 'was' instead of 'saw'?
- Can he or she read a word once but then get it wrong further down the page?
- Does your child spell the same word in different ways?
- Is he or she poor at concentrating on reading and writing?
- Does your child often confuse left and right and have problems with time?
- Can he or she easily answer questions out loud but finds it difficult to write those answers?
- Is your child often very clumsy?
- Does he or she have trouble recognising different sounds in words or words that rhyme?

What if my child is highly able or gifted?

With gifted or highly intelligent children there is sometimes a mismatch between their needs and what the school has to offer. It is important to identify a highly able child as soon as possible so that both school and home can be as supportive as possible.

- Many gifted children learn to read early, often before going to school.
- They often read a great deal, very quickly and have a large vocabulary.
- They always want to know the 'how' and 'why' of things.
- They can work on their own at an earlier age and concentrate for longer.
- They have wide interests that they often follow up in great detail.
- They seem to have huge amounts of energy that can be wrongly thought of as hyperactivity.
- They get on well with adults.
- They like to learn new things and are highly inquisitive.
- They tackle their work in a very organised and efficient way.
- They really want to learn, find out or explore and are very persistent.
- They usually want to do work with no help.

Literacy in special schools

Children with the greatest learning difficulties attend special schools. If your child attends a special school he or she will be taught reading and writing in much the same way as in a mainstream school. The Literacy Hour is successfully taught in schools where children have severe learning and physical difficulties. Just as in a mainstream school your child will make progress over his or her entire school life and be well prepared for adult life.

Parent quote

"We talked to the school about Jane being highly able. She now joins an older class for part of the week and is much happier."

Glossary

Attainment Targets   Targets for children's learning in each subject at different stages. Each attainment target is divided into eight levels, like steps up a ladder.

Baseline Assessment   Teacher observation of children within the first seven weeks of entering the Reception class, which is used to assess learning levels in maths, English and social skills

Basic Grammar   A set of rules and guidelines to help us use language correctly.

Concrete poetry   Poems where the words are displayed in a way which represents or reflects what they describe.

Core subjects   The main subjects in the National Curriculum: English, maths and science. R.E. (religious education) and I.C.T. (Information and Communications Technology) are also treated like core subjects. These are the only subjects where set programmes of study have to be taught in full.

Dyslexia   A difficulty with processing written language, usually leading to quite severe problems with reading and writing. The causes of dyslexia and which children to include in the category lead to a lot of disagreement. Sometimes called word blindness or 'specific learning difficulties' though this also covers other conditions.

Foundation subjects   Subjects covered in schools as part of the National Curriculum which are not English, maths and science (the core subjects) or R.E. and I.C.T. These include history, geography, music, design technology, art and P.E.

Hand-eye co-ordination   Control of hand movements so that what is seen can be touched, manipulated or copied easily.

Information and Communications Technology (I.C.T.)   The term to replace I.T. (Information Technology) meaning the use of computers and other electronic means to enhance learning.

Information texts   Pieces of writing that inform, providing explanation.

Key Stages   Stages at which a child's education can be assessed, after following a programme of work. There are four Key Stages, dividing ages 5-7, 7-11, 11-14 and 14-16.

Literacy Hour   The time each day which schools have to devote to teaching literacy skills.

Local Education Authority (LEA)   The county, borough or district education authority. LEAs have many specific roles especially in admissions, finance and special educational needs.

Mirror writing   Writing which appears 'back to front' and can only be read by being reflected in a mirror.

National Curriculum   The government's system of education broken into four Key Stages, which applies to all pupils of compulsory school age in maintained schools. It contains core and foundation (non-core) subjects, and incorporates National Tests at the end of each Key Stage.

National Literacy Strategy Framework for Teaching   A clear set of instructions for teachers from Reception to Year 6 on how to teach reading and writing.

National Tests   Formerly known as SATS these tests are taken in school at the end of each Key Stage — at ages 7, 11 and 14 — to determine what Attainment Targets pupils have reached. The scores are also used, especially at age 11, to compare the results of schools as a whole.

OFSTED (Office for Standards in Education)   The government department that oversees inspections and sends teams to assess individual schools.

Phonics   Teaching or learning reading based on the sounds of letters.

Phonic knowledge   The ability to recognise the sounds that individual letters in a word will make.

Reading age   A standard of reading ability based on an average, measured in years and months.

Sentence level work   Grammar and punctuation work in the Literacy Hour.

Teacher assessment   The teacher's own judgements about the level of progress children have made. This is both a part of deciding what and how to teach, and also takes place more formally at set times, especially with the National Tests at 7 and 11 years old.

Text level work   Teaching comprehension and composition in the Literacy Hour using a book, poem, piece of information text or an extract from other writing.

Word level work   Phonics, spelling, vocabulary and handwriting work.

USEFUL INFORMATION

National Association for Special Educational Needs
NASEN House, 4/5 Amber Business Village
Amber Close, Amington, Tamworth B77 4RP
Web: www.nasen.org.uk
Phone: 01827 311 500

Basic Skills Agency
7th Floor, Commonwealth House
1-19 New Oxford Street, London WC1A 1NU
Web: www.basic-skills.co.uk/
Phone: 020 7405 4017
National development agency for basic literacy and numeracy skills.

National Confederation for Parent Teacher Associations (NCPTA)
2 Ebbsfleet Estate, Stonebridge Road, Gravesend, Kent DA11 9DZ
Web: www.rmplc.co.uk/orgs/ncpta
Phone: 01474 560 618
Promotes partnership between home and school, children, parents, teachers and education authorities.

Advisory Centre for Education (ACE)
Department A, Unit 1B Aberdeen Studios
22 Highbury Grove, London N5 2DQ
Web: www.ace-ed.org.uk/
Phone: 020 7354 8321
Free advice, information and support for parents of children in state schools.

DfEE (Department for Education and Employment)
Sanctuary Buildings, Great Smith Street, London SW1P 3BT
Web: www.dfee.gov.uk
Phone: 020 7925 5000
Free publications on all aspects of education can be sent out, available by phoning 01787 880 946

REACH (National Research Centre for Children with Reading Difficulties)
California Country Park, Nine Mile Ride, Finshampstead, Berkshire RG40 4HT
Web: www.reach-reading.demon.co.uk
Phone: 0118 973 7575
Fax: 0118 973 7105
For anyone caring for a child with a disability, illness or learning problem which affects their reading, language or communication.

The Book Trust
Book Trust House, 45 East Hill, London SW18 2QZ
Web: www.booktrust.org.uk/index.htm
Phone: 020 8516 2977
A charitable organisation that provides many services including book lists to help with book choosing.

The Federation of Children's Book Clubs
9 Westroyd, Pudsey, West Yorkshire LS28 8HZ
Phone: 0113 257 9950
A national voluntary organisation which aims to promote enjoyment and interest in children's books.

Anything Left-Handed
57 Brewer Street, London W1
Phone: 020 7437 3910
A shop specialising in equipment for left-handed people (such as scissors), with books on handwriting and other issues concerning left-handedness.

WEBSITES

www.standards.dfee.gov.uk/literacy
The Department for Education and Employment site. Provides access to lots of information and links to other websites.

www.dfee.gov.uk/sen/defn.htm
The government information site on special needs.

www.yearofreading.org.uk
The website of the National Year of Reading.

www.achuka.co.uk/index.html
Achuka offers information about children's books and the authors who write them with details of other sites.

www.basic-skills.co.uk/
The website of Basic Skills, who work with schools to develop basic skills.

www.ace-ed.org.uk/
The website of the Advisory Centre for Education.

www.hometown.aol.com/wiseowlsw
A UK children's specialist in education software to play online or download.

www.bbc.co.uk/education/schools/primary.shtml
Home and school learning resources for children. The BBC education site as a whole has resources to cover a large range of educational issues.

www.rmplc.co.uk/orgs/nagc/index.html
The National Association for Gifted Children site.

www.ed.uri.edu/smart/HOMEPAGE/lithp.htm
Links to other literacy sites organised by topic.

BOOKLIST

Reception fiction
The Very Hungry Caterpillar by Eric Carle (Penguin)
Reception non-fiction
Going to School by Anne Civardi (Usborne)

Year 1 fiction
Peace at Last by Jill Murphy (Macmillan)
Year 1 non-fiction
Colours (Dorling Kindersley)

Year 2 fiction
What Will Emily Do? by Gillian Cross (Mammoth)
Year 2 non-fiction
Big Bugs by Mary Gribbin (Ladybird)

Year 3 fiction
Diary of a Killer Cat by Anne Fine (Penguin)
Year 3 non-fiction
Kingfisher First Encyclopedia of Science (Kingfisher)

Year 4 fiction
Game of Catch by Helen Cresswell (Hodder)
Year 4 non-fiction
Nature at Risk by Sally Morgan (Kingfisher)

Year 5 fiction
Hacker by Malorie Blackman (Corgi)
Year 5 non-fiction
The War Years. The Home Front by Brian Moses (Wayland)

Year 6 fiction
The Lion, The Witch and the Wardrobe by C.S. Lewis (Collins)
Year 6 non-fiction
Anne Frank — The Diary of a Young Girl (Puffin)